The Berry-Picker House

A Novella

Mary Pierre Quinn-Stanbro

ISBN: 1544817665
ISBN-13: 978-1544817668

DEDICATION

This story is dedicated to Francis P. Quinn and Amelia (Molly) Shear – my parents.

They have inspired me in their own special ways to be all I can be, and I have faith they are smiling down on me and my family from heaven where they are together once again.

A portion of the proceeds from this book will go to:
Iron Island Museum, Buffalo, NY

ACKNOWLEDGEMENTS

With thanks to my cousin Kali Quinn at the Center for Compassionate Creativity for helping me realize the dream of sharing this story.

And gratitude for the group that recorded
my song *Lace Around the Moon*:

Katie Klein – Vocals
Mike Lettiere – Guitar
Michael Marcklinger – Recording/Mixing Engineer
Slade Templeton - Mastering Engineer
Recorded at: Elmwoodaudio.com

You can listen to the song here:

www.lacearoundthemoon.com

MARY PIERRE QUINN-STANBRO

CONTENTS

PREFACE

In 1998 my husband Gene purchased land in Naples, New York. With the property came a main house, a barn, and a berry-picker house. The purchase was unconventional; since he was not interested in moving into the house for quite some time, Gene agreed to let the owner of the home reside there until her death. This was a perfect arrangement for him since he was still working for a government agency in Buffalo and basically purchased the property for his retirement years.

I have been coming out to the "farm" for the past fourteen years. There are 28+ acres of breathtaking landscapes that change four times a year. Each rolling hillside is only more beautiful than the next, including thirteen acres that are filled with grapes. For the first three years I visited, rather than stay in the main house, we stayed in the berry-picker house – at first because the previous owner's mother was living there and then once she passed away Gene rented out the main house for a couple of years. Renting didn't work out, so when Gene moved to Philadelphia for a higher-graded position, the main house was left unattended. Knowing that he wouldn't be able to do anything with the farm until he retired was more difficult than he thought it would be – so much so that during his five years working in Philly he couldn't even bring himself to visit the farm except for a handful of times just to make sure the buildings were still standing.

Gene decided to rebuild the berry-picker house into a rustically livable condition. We didn't have running water but he installed electricity and a wood-burning stove, and most importantly, he added a composting toilet for me. This was all rather comical because prior to my years at the farm, many considered me to be "high-maintenance." My friends would ask me how I could stand to go out there under those conditions, but honestly I felt at peace out there. The scenery of Gene's grape farm perched high on a hill over-looking Canandaigua Lake was breathtaking. Gene got me believing in what he believed – someday this place was going to be spectacular.

Eventually we started to have friends and family come and stay in the berry-picker house. They also came to love the warmth and underdeveloped rustic charm of the place. The farm became the melting pot of used furniture donated by family and friends. Within a couple of years, it had become the place people wanted to go and experience at least once, especially in the warmer months – it is hard in the middle of the deep winter to put your boots and clothes on and go outside to the "shooney" (our outhouse).

Once Gene retired and began living full-time at the farm, he replaced the older, less popular Sheridan and Catawba grapes with Concords, and he started to restore the main house. The house has curved walls, curved wooden trim and molding, and original wooden shutters. It is a lot of work to gut and rebuild each room, but once complete, he hopes that the house will have the same original feel and splendor it must have had in its day so many years ago.

Gene now lives in the main house, and I continue to visit once a month until I retire and can join him permanently with the federal pension I have worked towards over the past thirty-one years.

We are making all these renovations with the thought process that after I retire, we may turn it into a small bed and breakfast or a wonderful place for family and friends to experience all that the land has to offer. We now refer to the place as "Gene-Pierre's."

The berry-picker house is left open for other family members and friends who come to visit us. There is more privacy at the berry-picker house than at the main house. Everyone seems to congregate more at the main house as it is larger and has running water and even has air conditioning! If people want to be alone and closer to nature, they usually stay down at the berry-picker house. It is quieter there, and you don't feel like you have to be part of all that is going on in the main house. You can just sit and relax on the deck looking out over the rolling hills and rows of grapes. It is so peaceful to simply sit and marvel at the beauty that is all around while taking in the smell of the grapes.

Whenever anyone comes to stay with us, we have them sign the walls that Gene built for the guest bedroom in the berry-picker house. This idea was inspired when we saw that the original walls in our bedroom had many signatures and messages left by the workers who had stayed at the berry-picker house during harvest seasons long ago. This wall always intrigued me: *What must their lives have been like? How was it to be away from their home for periods of time to go and do the difficult, back-breaking work of picking berries?"*

The weekend I wrote this story, Gene's daughter Megan and her friend came out to help us empty three of the rooms upstairs so that the electricity could be installed. While Gene was making them his famous crispy bacon, home-fried potatoes and the egg of choice, I went for my walk out the main road toward the little town of Cheshire. On my way back I was walking up to the house looking down into the vineyard, and I couldn't help but marvel at the beauty of the land and the unique structure of the little berry-picker house. It looks like a beacon in a storm – a guiding light drawing you in. Only the top of the building is really visible from the road, but when you walk down the little hill to get to it, you just feel like you are coming home to a safe haven. I started thinking of all the names on the wall and thought, "Boy, if those walls could talk, what a story they would tell…"

PROLOGUE

I found out about Phillip's arrest the morning when a letter arrived from his sister Anna. She didn't explain the whole story, but asked if I would be willing to come up to Naples for the duration of the upcoming trial. I hadn't heard from Phillip in many months, and now I understood why.   Something awful had happened.

"It would mean so much to Phillip to have a friendly face in the crowd when everyone will be looking at him with such disdain," she wrote. "Phillip appreciated the fact that you kept in constant contact with him through letter-writing all these years. He told me that you were the only other person besides me and Carmelita who accepted him."

Apparently Anna had been disowned by the entire town after Phillip was charged and she too needed a friend – someone in her and Phillip's court. She pleaded that I be the one to do this and offered to pay my way from New Orleans.

Maybe there was some way I could be of service to them, but I was getting up in age and hadn't traveled in quite some time. Wondering what trouble Phillip had gotten himself into, I took a walk through the Quarter to think it all through...

MARY PIERRE QUINN-STANBRO

CHAPTER 1

OUR ORIGINAL MEETING

"Laissez les bons temps rouler!"

That is how I would always start off each set of my shows while performing at jazz saloons or clubs throughout the city of New Orleans. It is a Cajun saying that means "Let the good times roll!" As the lead singer for a band called the Lagniappe Orchestra, I was the queen of the "good times" back in the day. I came up with the name for our band as I felt that we were giving our audience a "lagniappe" every time we performed – something given or obtained by way of good measure.

I was a fairly well known jazz singer in that early part of century - Maria Pierre Quinones - although people around town mostly referred to me by my stage name, Pierre. I made a decent living playing with my band around the Storyville and Tremé sections of the Crescent City. The actual wages I received for performing were not all that plentiful, but the free meals and drinks that were part of the package kept me going for several years. I was never someone who needed the finer things in life. I just wanted to share my words and voice with others who would appreciate it. For me this was self-actualization in its simplest form.

Now, I need you to understand that although I sang at different brothels throughout Storyville, the only thing I performed involved using my vocal cords to belt out jazz songs. I was not involved in what Storyville was known for in those years – being the red light district of New Orleans. The politicians during that time thought it would be best if they regulated prostitution and drugs, and yes, I was often asked if I would ever consider that type of "employment," but I always refused. I was fortunate to have a beautiful voice that enabled me to sing for my supper rather than having to do less reputable things. But I never judged the women who were working at the brothels. It was not an easy time for us. We were just trying to survive in whatever way we could. We were all respectful of each other and the choices we were forced to make.

The most beautiful brothel in Storyville was called Mahogany Hall, but Maison de Pierre on Basin Street was equally spectacular with its grand furnishings and beautiful courtyard draped with billowing ferns. It was only coincidental that the place I worked at shared my namesake. Perhaps that did help me get the job at this establishment. I was very fortunate to be working for Madam Gratia in this way. She was a fair woman and she was good to all of her girls.

No expense was spared at this house of ill repute. There was a grandiose fountain in the middle of the main room, which actually had champagne flowing out of it on New Year's Eve! Even more splendid than the fountain were the crystal chandeliers that hung in every room. They gave the entire house a feeling of opulence. The men who came to visit got what they were paying for served to them in exquisite surroundings. No wonder Madam Gratia's girls could charge up to ten dollars for the experience. Maison de Pierre was also referred to as an "Octoroon Hall" as it had prostitutes who were of mixed races providing their special services. Segregation was going on during this time but things were a little different in Storyville than other parts of New Orleans and the South. In the brothels here, the only color people were concerned with was the color of money. And a lot of money was being made.

I was the lead singer in our band but I was not able to do justice with the few instruments I could play. The gift of playing musical instruments was bestowed upon Jeremy. He was my piano player and he also played the trombone. He was exceptional and had made quite a name for himself around the District. The other thing Jeremy was known for was his eyes. They were stunning. No one could really tell what color they were as they shined like the crystals on the chandeliers throughout Maison de Pierre. That is how he got his stage name, "Jeremy Jewel." His eyes dazzled like fine jewels, and people couldn't help but stare at them.

We mostly performed songs that were made popular by other jazz artists but I was fortunate enough to have an original song too. The words for "Lace Around the Moon" came easily to me one night as I was sitting outside in my little courtyard staring up at the moon. I thought how remarkable it was that the leaves silhouetted the moon in such a way that it made it look like it was draped with lace. The lyrics came together that night and I immediately had my band put it to music. "Lace Around the Moon" became my signature song, and I performed it at every single show:

It all depends
On how you look at it

And what your mind's eye can see.
All I ask is that you'll think of me...

The moon is our connection.
With the leaves reflection,
I imagine seeing your face
Surrounded by the lace.

With every breath I take,
With every step I make,
I am always thinking of you.
I hope you see it too.

The north, the south, the east, the west
The crescent, new, the full, harvest...
The different phases of the moon
Bring back memories of you.

Our love sometimes seems to wane
From all the heartache and the pain.
At times we went our separate ways
But that was just a passing phase.

The leaves illuminate,
The moon then creates,
This illusion in the sky
As the seasons go by.

The shadows are made
With the sunlight they fade.
I look up and I see
And wonder how can it be...

The ins, the outs, the ups, the downs
The highs, the lows, the smiles, the frowns,
The times filled with chaotic scenes...
I never could forget our dreams.

Our love sometimes seems to wane
From all the heartache and the pain
At times we went our separate ways
But that was just a passing phase

Whenever you look up
And see the lace around the moon,
Know that our hearts will be together soon.
With this, we will never be apart.

One evening, just as I finished up my first set with this song, a young man approached me and respectfully asked if he could talk to me about my music. He commented on my beautiful shimmering green dress adorned with three strands of glass beads. He said the light beams coming off them made it appear as though I had a magical, mystical aura around me. I was quite surprised by how young he was but he was totally sincere in his request for my time. I had ten minutes before my next set and he had already paid enough attention to know that I would gladly welcome a whiskey, neat, which he offered when he first approached me. He wanted to know more about "Lace Around the Moon." "The words are so simple, yet so beautiful," I remember him saying, "They speak right to my heart."

I responded that the words did the same for me, and that this song was to help loved ones who were separated from each other: "Whenever you look up and see the lace around the moon, know that our hearts will be together soon."

He introduced himself as Phillip and went on to tell me that he heard a jazz singer for the first time a year before at a hotel where he was from in Naples, New York. The sound of jazz immediately moved him unlike any other music he had ever heard before. After that night, Phillip couldn't shake the feeling of his familiarity with the music and he felt compelled to hear the real thing and experience it first-hand, so he saved up his money and decided to take a trip to New Orleans to experience jazz and some of the other interesting things that were going on in our city. He said he felt he "deserved this treat" because after this adventure, he was heading off to law school.

I asked him questions about what it was like to live in New York and I learned that there was much more than just New York City. I learned that his family owned a berry and grape farm back in Central New York. He said that jazz music was something he could get lost in. That it took him to another place and time. He needed this imaginary escape to get through the monotonous never-ending work on their family farm at home. He felt he belonged and longed for the place where it all came from.

That this teenager could relate to all the songs we performed intrigued me. In connecting with him I felt like I was looking into the eyes of an old soul. He wanted to know about the roots of jazz music and if I could just tell him about New Orleans – the way I was living it. He said he would gladly pay me for my time as he realized it wasn't conducive to have longer conversations between my sets.

I was taken aback by his unusual request, but the thought of some extra cash on hand was very enticing. I was off on Mondays so I told him I could take him around for the day and show him some of the places that he might enjoy. I did, however, put a stipulation on our outing. I said I would only agree to go if my band-mate Jeremy would accompany us. I felt much more comfortable with another male being present when we were going around the District. It wasn't that I felt Phillip would be inappropriate towards me, but I just didn't want to have to worry about any improprieties.

I knew that Jeremy was also off on Monday so I asked him if he would be willing to go around with us. He originally chuckled at the proposition but when Phillip pulled out his billfold and gave each of us twenty dollars as a goodwill gesture and offered to pay us fifty dollars each for the tour, we both politely shook his hand and made a plan to meet in front of Mahogany Hall on Monday morning at ten - keep in mind, nothing ever happens too early in the Crescent City. I told Phillip if we were going to do this, we were going to do it right and that meant we would be going to places called "Social Aids" or "Pleasure Clubs." This was where the real jazz was being made and played. He agreed and we all parted ways. I had a feeling I knew what Phillip was going to be doing for the rest of the evening, but that was his business.

On Monday, Phillip arrived promptly with a smile on his face. "Laissez les bons temps rouler," he shouted, and the three of us were on our way.

We were quite a sight to be seen around town that day. Here I was, a woman around thirty years older than Phillip, taking him into places he most likely would not have been welcome were it not for the fact that he was with us. Jeremy and I were well accepted and respected amongst the brothel owners, saloonkeepers, and the patrons, as they had known us through our music for years.

What a day we had! Phillip said it was like experiencing "a feast for the senses." The smell of all of the food simmering in different pots through the District and being served in the different Social Aid clubs continued to allure him. He had never tasted food like gumbo or jambalaya before, let alone a crawfish boil. The sounds of the jazz music he heard throughout the day and night was like nothing he had ever experienced before. Although jazz did not originate in Storyville, it was predominantly the music that was being played. The music was everywhere and never-ending.

"It eases my mind," I remember Phillip saying as we listened to song after song. What his eyes and ears were taking in was enough to create a lifetime of memories for him, and his sense of touch had also been stimulated beyond his comprehension. The things he was touching and feeling? Well, that was a private matter.

In the early evening we went to Frank Early's "My Place" saloon and heard pianist Tony Jackson tickle the ivories unlike Phillip had ever heard until this moment. Jelly Roll Morton and Buddy Bolden also made special appearances. Although Phillip had never heard of these performers, he was quite impressed, especially when they performed "Jelly Roll Blues." We stayed there for a couple of hours taking it all in. By that time, it was just past eleven, and all three of us were exhausted from our full day of carousing. Phillip couldn't thank us enough and paid us our agreed-upon fee plus a twenty-dollar tip. This was far more than we had ever made in a good week of playing music!

Phillip had thought he had become quite knowledgeable about New Orleans by reading all he could find on his visits to the library. But he admitted reading about something is quite different than experiencing it. "I see now that I needed to live it to fully love and appreciate it," he commented at the end of that night. He was surprised by how much of an impact Mardi Gras (Fat Tuesday) had on the entire culture. He saw how everyone he made contact with that day was focused on their preparation for the upcoming Mardi Gras season. He knew that the beads (or "throws," as some people referred to them) were said to bring luck for the upcoming year. He said he had so much fun during this time with us that he never needed to experience Mardi Gras. That this was his Mardi Gras. He told us that the one thing he would always remember about his New Orleans experience was the abundance of colors. He couldn't believe how all aspects of everyday living were incorporated into three symbolic colors – purple for justice, green for faith and gold for power. A good time was had by all and would never be forgotten by Phillip. He continued to write to me in letters over the years that his time spent with me that day was "the most memorable of his whole life."

Before we parted from each other, I reached out to shake Phillip's hand but instead he boldly kissed my hand, placed it on his heart, and much to my surprise, he repeated the words of my song: "Whenever I look up and see the lace around the moon, know that our hearts will be together soon."

I took off the three strands of glass beads I had worn around my neck for years and gave them to Phillip as a parting gift.

And I hadn't seen him since.

CHAPTER 2

PHILLIP'S STORY

During the four months before the trial, I stayed at the main house on the Wilcox property. It was quite a beautiful place. Very different from New Orleans, of course, but just like Phillip had described in his letters all those years.

Each morning after breakfast, Anna would take me to meet with Phillip at the local jail where he was being held. Although he had aged into quite a weary man over the years, I could still see a flicker of that bright-spirited teenager living inside him.

In our new time together, I became his confidant. It was apparent that he hadn't told me the full truth in his letters and that he needed to unburden his tormented soul of all his sins and indiscretions. Little by little he filled in more of the details of his life story, which I now impart to you:

Phillip's parents, Henry and Lillian Wilcox of Naples, were berry farmers – very prosperous berry farmers. People from all around Canandaigua Lake would come to the Wilcox farm to purchase their delectable berries. Although the main use was for dying clothing, local juice-pressing houses would also process the berries for pies and jams, and even some for homemade wine. The Wilcox's always dreamed of the day when they would have children to love and leave their vineyard to. By the time the couple reached their thirties and were still without a son or daughter they assumed it was simply God's will and they planned on living their lives content with each other, tending to their berries and their thriving vineyard. It always seems to be when you least expect things that they happen. Not only were they blessed with one child but two. They had twins – a boy they named Phillip and a girl they named Anna.

Henry and Lillian were good parents and gave their children a loving, nurturing home. The twins were not identical in any way. They were polar opposites both in their physical appearance and in their personalities. What God did not bestow on Phillip in terms of height, he did grant to Anna. She was taller than most of the other girls in school and remained so through adulthood. Anna had a beautiful complexion with a captivating smile. She was sweet, but she wasn't a pushover by any means. Her brother, Phillip, was above average looking but below average in height. He had a muscular build and the years of constantly walking, lifting, pulling out vines, and pounding posts around the vineyard helped to keep him in good shape. He wore the results of this physical activity well. It was very important to him that people, especially females, saw him as good-looking. His smaller stature did not stop his ego from growing. When people met Phillip they were impressed by him, and this was important to him. He always wanted to be noticed. The opposite was true for Anna. While she was equally as easy on the eyes as Phillip, she did not need to have all eyes on her. She was very secure in herself. While she took pride in her appearance, she did not need constant accolades.

It was hard to believe that these two were twins and had been raised by the same parents when they were so different in their own perceptions of their self-worth.

Anna didn't need to prove self-worth – it came from inside her, whereas Phillip needed others to boost his self-esteem because that was somehow missing from within him. By all appearances, the twins were well adjusted and happy as teenagers can be. They had a very decent life and both of them were on their way to becoming successful young adults. However, what people let be seen and what comes through on the outside is quite different than what is actually going on within.

Phillip continued to be quite insecure but he never let that be obvious to anyone – anyone other than Anna. After all, she was his twin. They had been together right from the start, and had a special bond that only they could understand. Anna knew Phillip's strengths and weaknesses. She loved her little brother and let him be what he needed to be. At the same time in her heart she knew that something was not quite right with some of Phillip's thought processes or his actions. But nevertheless, she hoped for the best – that he would grow out of some of his bad habits, especially his extreme temper tantrums. Unfortunately for Anna, and especially for Phillip, that never happened. If things didn't go his way, Phillip would get mad and lash out at whoever or whatever was standing in his way.

As they grew up, Anna loved getting involved in the family business and had a good grasp on the daily farm management. Phillip, on the other hand, while enjoying the comforts that his family's business provided him with, had less and less interest in the berry business and began thinking he was above the "menial" farming. In school he played sports, received good grades, and the young ladies were all attracted to his quick wit and the Wilcox family name.

Phillip was very bright in school, especially in science,

and he loved learning about the law and working with numbers. By nature, Phillip was argumentative and relentless when trying to prove his point. He never gave up on an argument. He was able to articulately debate anyone who disagreed with him and he usually won the argument through sheer determination. He could get anyone to come around to his way of thinking. He saw the law was black and white, right and wrong and was ready to deal in shades of gray, so at an early age he decided he would go to college to become a tax attorney.

His parents saw his talents and aspirations and saved up money so they could send him to college to get a law degree. Although they were considered well off in the farming arena, they still required Phillip to spend his time after school working on the berries. They told him if he did his part on the farm and kept his grades up at school, they would pay for his college education in Buffalo, New York at the University of Buffalo's Law School. Since he had no other way to pay for school, he knew this was going to be his only way out of the family berry-farming business.

Phillip was a master manipulator and did exactly what he needed to do to get what he wanted, especially when it came to anything he was told he couldn't have. Things that came too easily for him were not as enticing. Such was the case of a beautiful young French girl at school named Danielle, who was rather smitten with the feisty Phillip. He kept up appearances of being a proper young man who was dating the proper Danielle but that was just for show. He was never anything other than respectable to Danielle but that relationship did not "thrill" him. Even at that young age he liked to walk on the wild side. Phillip was very much into sex but he pushed all of that down when he was with Danielle. If he had proposed anything improper, she would have told her parents, and then his secret might be revealed.

Phillip would take Danielle out on dates to local diners, dances, and the silent movies. Of course, with all of the attention he was showing her, she assumed that the relationship was really going somewhere. She would make sure to be at all of the functions he might attend, she cheered him on at every sporting event, and she eagerly tried to weasel her way into any conversation he was engaged in. He didn't detest Danielle, but he did not plan on any type of future with her. There wasn't the challenge, the chase. He needed to be in control of any and all situations, and when young girls and later women would go about enticing him into their webs, where they were in control, he didn't run: he nonchalantly sidestepped this very sticky entanglement. He was not going to get caught in that spider's web!

During Phillip and Anna's high school years, their parents would hold dances for young people at the Naples Hotel. They wanted their children to have a wonderful social upbringing. They didn't flaunt their money, but being intelligent business people, the only food they ever served was berry tarts, pies and juices. Anna met Peter Ellis, a man from the nearby town of Geneva whose family had even more money than the Wilcox's. Peter seemed to adore Anna from the moment they met at one of these dances. She was a wonderful dancer and carried herself with pride and dignity. This was very appealing to Peter. He knew that someday his family's electrical engineering business would become his own, and he wanted a woman who could be his partner both in the business and in life – someone who shared his same values and beliefs. He wanted a "lady," and that was exactly what Anna was.

Henry and Lillian were very happy to allow their

daughter to date this young man because he came from such a well-respected family. Peter took the train from Geneva to Naples to visit Anna at the Wilcox home on weekends. While he was there, Peter would go hunting for deer and rabbit with Phillip. Hunting was the only interest they shared, and Phillip was rather cruel in his hunting techniques. It was not the sport of the game for him or the practical use of the meat; it was the destruction of inferior life that was the thrill. Peter became suspect of Phillip's questionable behavior, and he didn't want to get involved in anything that might upset Anna because he wanted a future with her. He remained a gentleman with his main focus being to make Anna happy, and since Anna doted on Phillip, Peter tolerated him as best he could.

Phillip, Peter, and Anna would spend a lot of time together especially at the different dances throughout Naples and sometimes they all went to Canandaigua. One particular night at the Naples Hotel, there was an Al Jolson impersonator with his band performing jazz songs in blackface. Phillip had never seen such a thing and just sat there staring at the performer, seemingly under a spell. Although he didn't think of himself as a deeply emotional person, the music touched him. He said it enveloped him, reaching into his heart and soul. The music was not well received by the general crowd that evening. These were mostly farmers and proper church-going people after all, and this new type of music was simply not part of their traditional values. But to Phillip, it was the most wonderful sound he had ever heard. The performer stayed on afterwards to tell stories of the "Crescent City." Phillip sat enthralled, listening to the performer's incredible stories, and he envisioned himself going to this special place to listen to the jazz music and eat the beignets and jambalaya. Most of all, he wanted to experience what Storyville had to offer. From the next day forward, he started to save his money so he could go to New Orleans.

CHAPTER 3

RUNNING OF THE GRAPES

As Phillip continued on, I heard things I wish I hadn't, but I didn't let him see the true feelings I was experiencing. I never flinched. Not even once. I just took it all in, and he said that it was the greatest gift he had ever received:

To the Wilcox's, everything revolved around harvesting their berries and the grapes. They hired many berry-pickers to do the repetitious, backbreaking picking and, being decent people, they let these workers stay in their berry-picker house so they wouldn't have to travel back and forth from the local towns or faraway cities where they lived. Yes, they were doing the workers a favor but they were also "protecting their investments."

The berry-picker house was built around the turn of the century and served the purpose of keeping the workers warm and dry, but that was about it. The inside was framed in oak and the outside was made of pine. The house was approximately forty feet long by twenty feet wide with four rooms and an outhouse nearby. The house was sparsely furnished but it was functional, and that was the important thing to the Wilcox's. The room farthest to the east side had a wood-burning stove and a table with chairs. This was usually where the berry-pickers would quickly eat their meals in two shifts. The men and women slept separately in the next two rooms of four cots each. Everyone kept their supplies in the remaining room, and the foreman slept outside of the dining room so he could keep an eye on his co-workers.

For a couple of months out of the year, this was home to the berry-pickers. It was where they sought shelter and where they found comfort, spending many hours talking about their lives back home. When the first group of berry-pickers who stayed there signed the wall with their names and little messages in the first room in the house, this became an established custom. A kind of marking of territory – or at least having some piece of themselves left behind for others to acknowledge.

With the summers and autumns of the harvesting season going by, Phillip was growing up and as his hormones raged, he became more and more sexually curious. Until he could get to New Orleans himself, Phillip decided that he would turn the berry-picker house into his own little Storyville where he could partake in his own lagniappe – a little something extra he said he felt "entitled to." He felt this type of behavior was acceptable since the girls were working for his family and staying in their berry-picker house. Referring to the young women who worked on his parents' farm as "BB's," berry babes, his main focus became to help himself to the "sweetest of the berries."

He spent a great deal of his time trying to entice the fairer sex into his fold. But he was very suave and debonair about it. He would offer to give the young BB's a ride around town in his new Ford Model T. He would take one out on a Friday evening to Grimes Glen and while sitting at the waterfalls, he would tell her how pretty and special she was. On the way home he would pull over to offer her a drink and they would talk a bit until he found the perfect moment to kiss her. If things went well for Phillip, he admitted that he would touch her breast and maybe even pet her private parts. Usually, he said, that was as far as these young ladies were willing to go. Unfortunately that left him with his stick shift ready and raring to go.

Phillip was smart enough to know that he should never force himself further on the BB's (Terry, Angela, Phyllis, Esther, Kay, Marlene, Little Terry and Josephine). They liked the special attention he would show them. For these berry-picking young women, the work at the farm was at times backbreaking and repetitious but they were not treated badly. They had the backdrop of the most beautiful glens imaginable to work in all day. They were out in the fresh air and were able to chat amongst themselves. They weren't stuck inside dingy buildings like the sweatshops in New York City where some of their relatives were working.

These women had their freedom and they would all talk amongst themselves about what happened on these special rides with Phillip and laugh and giggle, as it was "only" just teenage petting. They felt that since they were young and not in love, it was better to be looked over than overlooked. This was the case until one day when Phillip offered to take GG out for a ride. He met his match with this one. She wasn't the prettiest of the BB's, but she was the smartest and she was just as sexually adventurous as Phillip. When he took her for the first ride, she not only let him touch her private parts, but she was the one who initiated "doing even more petting." Well, this was all Phillip needed to think that there could be more goodies in store for him with this girl. He knew she would be leaving when the first harvest was over, so he convinced her to come back for the second harvest. He was set on having more sexual experiences with her.

Once she returned, Phillip orchestrated what he called the "Running of the Grapes," so that he could get more time alone with GG. In order to get away with his shenanigans, he figured the safest thing to do was to invite all of the berry-pickers who stayed at the berry-picker house to participate in these late Friday evening adventures. By then, they all needed a break and something fun to do. At midnight, some participants would strip down naked on the top of the hill. Most of the young BB's didn't want to do it naked, but GG was glad to entice Phillip with her young, firm body. Next, Phillip gave everyone a cup filled with the "drink of the evening" and then they would take off running down to the pond and back. The game went that whoever had most of their drink left in their cup would win a prize of their choosing. Phillip kept a stockpile of blankets, pillows, canned goods, cigarettes, alcohol, and a special expensive concoction that would remove the severe purplish and red stains that came from picking the berries and grapes up in the rafters of the barn – a place where he knew his father would not venture.

In reality, the only similarity to the Running of the Bulls in Pamplona, Spain and his Running of the Grapes was that there was running involved. No fatalities occurred as a result of the Running of the Grapes, just some brush-burned or pricker-filled buttocks and legs. The biggest difference was that Phillip did not require the participants to be at least 18 years old – he liked the younger girls. At the running of the bulls, you cannot incite the bulls and you cannot be under the influence of alcohol. Phillip's main goal was to get them all incited and under the influence of alcohol. No one was forced to participate but the lure of going to the barn and picking out a prize of their choosing gave them the strength or desire to go along with his manipulative venture. He always knew exactly what he was doing and the participants agreed that what happened at the farm and the berry-picker house stayed at the farm and the berry-picker house.

On one of these second-harvest weekends after a Running of the Grapes, whether they won or not, he told all of the berry-pickers to go and wait for him in the barn where they could all pick a prize and that there was even more liquor waiting for them. He had been thinking ahead and hoped that this would be the night he had GG. He didn't even have to entice her. It was she who had Phillip! When the workers were all on their way down to the barn, she took Phillip by the hand and led him to her cot. They did not make love but they had sex. It was the first of many times they would use each other for what they each desired most.

As it turns out, GG had one up on Phillip, and it was a big one. She had listened to all of the BB's chattering and gossiping about how Phillip was always trying to get down their pants and how they wouldn't let him. She started thinking why should she have to live out her life as a berry-picker. She hated the impoverished life she was living. The little shack her family lived in embarrassed her, and she knew that she would never go to college to get an education. There just wasn't any money for that; there was hardly enough money for food. It all became clear to her that she wanted so much more for herself, and she saw that her way out was by letting Phillip "in."

During his senior year, Phillip appeared to be living two separate lives. During the week he would "properly" date Danielle, and on the weekends, he would "improperly" do GG. Even though Phillip spent a great deal of time with both of these girls, it did not stop him from doing extremely well in high school and graduating with honors. He had one summer left to get his fill of what he craved most at the farm and to go on his adventure to New Orleans, before he pursued his law degree.

This double life went on right up until he left for law school. Since he did not love either of these young women, it was easy for him to simply say goodbye to them and leave them behind. He never promised either of them anything. They were both "disposable," he said. "Why should he owe them anything, especially his love?" He was not even sure what love was. And after all, he saw himself as Phillip Wilcox who was on his way to bigger and better things. Both Danielle and GG knew this day would come when he left for college. Danielle was devastated, as she truly did love Phillip. She had hoped to one day be his wife. She had asked him if they could still continue to date and see each other on holidays or the summers when he would be coming back home. But Phillip wanted nothing to do with keeping up the pretense of a false relationship. He saw his time away at school as a way to break his ties with her. He told her that his time back home would be very limited as he planned to stay on in Buffalo during the summers and get a part-time job either at the college or in the area at a law firm so he could gain experience in his field. He said it wouldn't be fair to her to keep her hanging on, as he was not planning on a future with her. He never said it to her but Danielle had reached her expiration date. As for GG's feelings regarding Phillip's departure, it was never even discussed. What Phillip didn't know was that GG was ready to move on with her own plans and dreams.

In the six years that followed, Phillip received his undergraduate degree in business and then continued onto law school at the University of Buffalo. During his years in college, he never had a steady girlfriend. To his credit, he spent most of his time studying and had little time for dating. He preferred to not have anything more than sexual trysts with somewhat not-so-reputable women. To him sex was just sex; he was never willing to invest the time needed to cultivate a meaningful relationship.

Graduating with a concentration in tax law, Phillip toyed with the idea of working for a law firm in Buffalo where he had some relatives, but because he wouldn't have had the same name recognition there, instead he decided to work for a law firm specializing in tax law on the corner of Ontario and Main Streets in Canandaigua.

Shortly after Phillip graduated from law school and he began to work at the law firm in Canandaigua, his parents were killed in an automobile accident. Although he wasn't particularly close to his parents, he did respect them and truly mourned their passing. They were on their way into town for their regular Sunday church service. The roads were so slippery from the water coming off the Lake. They weren't even traveling at a high rate of speed when their automobile hit a patch of ice and went over the embankment. Both of their necks were broken from the accident. A month after the funeral of his parents, their will was read. The entire Wilcox farm and all of the buildings, the business and all of the stocks and bonds were to be equally divided between Anna and Phillip. Since Phillip wanted nothing to do with the farm, Anna paid him $40,000 to buy him out of his inheritance. The only other stipulation involved a one-time disbursement of $10,000 to someone with the initials A.C. Both Anna and Phillip insisted that their long-time family attorney, Charles Watkins, who was also the executor of the will, disclose who this was. However, since he was being paid handsomely for his services and he had signed a legally binding document stating that he would not divulge this information, he wasn't going to give it up – Charles was never one do anything to risk his payday.

Although Phillip had many flaws, no one could ever say that he wasn't ambitious. Quite the contrary – he was very driven and he felt a need to succeed wherever he could. At this point in his life, Phillip focused on working hard to establish himself as a well-respected tax attorney. However, now here he was in his large home on Chapel Street all alone, and he became very lonely. Perhaps it was that loneliness and the sudden death of his parents that made Phillip seek out a more secure home life. With his parents gone and with no real friends besides Peter and Anna, Phillip realized he should take a wife and become a "proper family man." He felt the pressure to grow up and move on with his life. He could no longer get away with his childish, boyhood antics of trying to get any and all girls to be with him.

Anna and Peter married while Phillip was away at law school. Upon returning, he decided to turn to them and their circle of "proper people" for his dating pool. Anna was happy to find her twin a wife because she thought it would make Phillip more grounded and respectable. She had heard all the whispers around town about Phillip and his questionable behavior but she chose to believe that it was nothing more than "idle gossip."

In his spare time on weekends, Phillip would visit Peter's family estate, and they would go to dances and parties – it was, after all, the Roaring Twenties. Phillip was a dapper dresser, an articulate conversationalist and a definite catch. Phillip didn't have to look very far for a date. Peter had a sister named Florence. He had met her a few times at different events or parties that the Ellis family hosted at their family estate when Anna and Peter first started dating. She was older so he never actually set his sights on her before; their families would have frowned upon the age difference. Besides, he had heard she was dating a serviceman while he was away at college. On the few occasions he had met her, she never seemed to acknowledge Phillip's existence. He was just her kid brother's friend.

However, watching her one night at one of their parties, he gave Florence a second glance and then a third.... She was the life of the party and no party was complete without her. People called her "Easy Flo" but it had nothing to do with her being sexually promiscuous. On one particular evening out at a local pavilion, she gave into Phillip's advances. She had been drinking away her sorrows to get over her serviceman boyfriend meeting a young French woman overseas.

Phillip perceived their sexual encounter as a statement of her desire to be with him on a somewhat permanent basis, but she was just drunk and lonely. He pursued her relentlessly after that. Flo saw their one night of sex as a one-night stand and she wouldn't give him the time of day or night for the next couple of weeks. And that was exactly what Phillip needed – the chase. "I always wanted what I couldn't have," he reminded me, "I loved the challenge." He felt he had to succeed at these conquests as if to make up for his "shortcomings." It was more of the challenge and the chase than actual love for Florence. Since he was now an adult, dating her was not so taboo. Florence eventually broke down and realized her younger years were falling behind her. If she were an unmarried woman by the age of thirty, she would be considered an "old maid." This sentiment, along with the fact that Florence didn't get her menses that month or the next, sealed the deal.

The two married two months after that at the Naples Hotel. Florence and Phillip did not live together before they married. Had they tested those waters, he would have realized that Florence was not just drowning her sorrows when she conceived; she was always drowning her sorrows from sun up to sundown. It was a topic that wasn't really discussed but rather whispered about. Unfortunately, Phillip didn't hear all the whispers – Florence was a full-blown alcoholic. That is why they called her Easy Flo – the drinks just continuously flowed down her throat. Her drink of choice was vodka on the rocks and she continued to drink these "ice waters" throughout her rough pregnancy. Subsequently, the child growing inside her alcohol-infused womb couldn't handle Florence's poor habits. Florence literally drank her baby, Phillip's baby, to death. Peter and Anna were devastated that Flo did such a thing when they hadn't yet been able to conceive.

After the tragedy of losing this child, Phillip never looked at Florence again with anything other than disdain and she was relieved. Their marriage was a marriage in name only. He didn't want to divorce her at this point since he was just starting his professional career and the stigma that went with divorces in that day and age was more than he was willing to risk. They agreed to have a marriage of "convenience." For Phillip this meant he was free to discreetly engage in "sex-capades" with "unethical women" as long as they were not from a reputable family and outside of a fifty-mile radius of Canandaigua. After all, Flo was the wife of the highly respected Phillip Wilcox, Esquire, and she was not going to let some other woman upstage her – she couldn't handle that. But if he chose to sleep around with low-lives where none of her family, friends or social acquaintances would know what he was up to, all the better… as long as she wasn't the one being injected with his seed.

They continued on with their loveless marriage for several years. Phillip was working hard, and Flo was hardly working at anything other than getting intoxicated daily. They still went on as though they had a solid marriage, at least for the sake of her parents. Phillip and Flo rarely spoke to each other when they were both home. And if they did, it would usually turn into a battle over something, usually her drinking. One holiday season the Ellis family invited Phillip and Flo to come and stay with them between the week of Christmas and the New Year. The day after Christmas, everyone had quite a few cocktails before heading out to dinner at a local restaurant. And before these cocktails, of course Flo had already had a couple of her ice waters. Once they were all seated to dinner, Flo became belligerent with Phillip for being overly friendly to the hostess. He didn't want to cause a scene in front of his in-laws so he just apologized and said that he had been a bit tipsy and perhaps out of line. He didn't make any more small talk with the hostess, and they were able to get through the uncomfortable dinner.

When they all returned to the Ellis home for a nightcap, things escalated. Flo started screaming at Phillip in front of everyone. He was humiliated by her behavior and what she was saying so he took her onto the back veranda, where Flo told him that she purposely drank during her pregnancy so she wouldn't have to bear a child with someone as vile as Phillip. She went on and on and started insulting him. Phillip was overcome with rage. Flo started flinging her fists at Phillip who lost it and shoved her backwards with enough force to break the wooden railing, causing her to topple over the side of the veranda. Thankfully, there was a good foot of snow that broke her fall.

Landing in the cold snow, she couldn't believe what just happened. She was so drunk that she just lay there and started screaming for her parents: "Come help me! Phillip just tried to kill me!"

Fast-thinking Phillip ran back into the house yelling, "Please hurry up and come outside and help me get Flo up

33

off the ground and back into the house. She is so drunk she fell backwards over the railing."

At that point, it was Phillip's word against Flo's. Her parents sided with Flo but knew that her drinking had something to do with her fall. Flo wanted to call the police and report the incident. However, her parents thought that would not look good to the neighbors or anyone else who might hear of what happened. They calmed Flo down and got her off to bed without Phillip. After that evening, her parents never much cared for him. In their eyes, from that moment forward, there was always a cloud of suspicion around Phillip. After all, he could have seriously harmed their only daughter. And as for Flo, she may have been drunk, but she knew that Phillip could have killed her that night if there hadn't been snow. She calmed down the next day and told Phillip she was not going to report the incident to the police, but that Phillip was going to pay for his misdeed. And when she said pay, she meant with his money. She liked money and the comforts that came with his money. Phillip did not want word of this incident to get back to his clients in Canandaigua, so he agreed to what she requested, and from that moment on, she had him by the billfold and by the family jewels.

CHAPTER 4

Before Carmelita

The more I heard, the more I felt torn. What a complex web was being woven. How could anything good ever come from it?

Phillip's career continued to thrive and he was becoming quite the man about town. Since he was a tax attorney and good at keeping his client's secrets, word spread. He was saving a lot of high-powered/high-profile people from tax consequences, and they were rewarding him handsomely. He was becoming very well versed in stocks and bonds and making quite a nice little nest egg for himself in a relatively short period of time. His business and financial life flourished. He still owned half of the stocks and bonds his parents had left him. He was on the fast track to bigger and better things. He never was going to return to the life of a farmer – or so he thought.

The stock market crash of 1929 was a pivotal moment that changed Phillip's life, as it did many other Americans. The crash was devastating for Phillip. All of his clients were wiped out financially. They no longer had money to invest so there were no legal issues with their investments. He was able to milk out six months at the law firm, but they could no longer afford his salary after that. The other issue for Phillip was that he and Anna were planning on their parents' stocks and bonds to take care of them financially in their retirement years, but after the crash, that well had dried up. There was only one thing left for Phillip to do: ask Anna if he could come back to the farm and to become the thing he dreaded most – a berry farmer. Even though he had already sold his share of the farm to Anna, and taken the $40,000 from her, Anna gave him the title of "farm owner." But at this point, he knew he was really just a hired hand.

Phillip had to go back home and "eat humble berry pie" with Flo in tow. I wondered why Flo would continue to stay with Phillip and not go back to live with her parents. He explained to me that her parents would never have understood her drinking and would probably have had her committed to a place so that she could sober up. To her, that would have been worse than having to live with Phillip. Her drinking was her world and she didn't want to have that taken away from her no matter what. So she stayed with Phillip and their marriage of convenience trailed on. Phillip stayed with her, as he knew that her family still had money even after the crash. He liked that bit of security especially since he didn't know if he would even be able to make any money back at the farm.

These were uncertain times for everyone. It didn't make sense to me but that was the choice the two of them made. They did not love each other but were caught in a trap that neither of them could break out of.

Phillip reluctantly settled into his new situation. He worked the farm, ate, slept and did his best to avoid Flo – not much of an existence for someone who should have been above such a menial life. During his first year back at the farm, he was very busy. Prohibition was still in effect. While it was illegal to manufacture and sell alcohol, Section 29 of the Volstead Act allowed wine and cider to be made at home from fruit. Phillip was allowed to make up to 200 gallons of wine, and that is what he did – in addition to growing the grapes and berries for jams and non-alcoholic juices. He was illegally selling the wine under the table for a large profit.

During Prohibition, there were two sides to the issue: you were either considered a "dry" (supported the movement) or a "wet" (not so much). Keep in mind, it is one thing when you are talking morality, but it is another thing when you are talking money or your livelihood. At the Wilcox farm, things were wet. Phillip liked that he was at least making some money. Nothing compared to the years back in Canandaigua when he was working as a tax attorney, but he at least had some cash on hand for when he would go to social events in Naples or Canandaigua. Those were somewhat limited times but he would make appearances at special functions. He would usually go with Anna and Peter, and when necessary, he took Flo. Phillip made it very clear to her that she still had to pull it together and sometimes go with him to keep up the pretense of a marriage or should I say "a mirage." She was also expected to keep the house clean and cook for him. As was their agreement back in Canandaigua: she could drink herself into a stupor each night and he could still get his fill of what he wanted most of all. He would usually travel to Buffalo to get those matters taken care of. Buffalo was thriving at that time. There were plenty of speakeasies and there were other things there that were also "easy." He so enjoyed going to Buffalo; it was a much larger city than Naples or Canandaigua. It was more cosmopolitan and had a thriving downtown area where jazz was even being played! He would relive his time in New Orleans down on Main Street in Buffalo. He needed these special trips to help get him through the daily grind of farm management. The jazz music would ease his mind, if even only for a night.

The berry-pickers would arrive at the beginning of July and work until the first week of August during the first harvesting of the berries. They would return from the second week in September until mid October or even a week later depending on how the weather that year affected the ripening of grapes for the second harvest. Phillip met with the berry-pickers when they arrived, set the rules, and explained what was expected of them. He was in charge and wanted them to know that. He also wanted them to all understand how fortunate they were to be working at the Wilcox farm and staying at the berry-picker house when there were food wars going on throughout the country. The berry-pickers were given a meal at around ten in the morning and then another meal at seven at night. They were given a roof over their heads and they were paid a salary. Phillip felt they should be grateful to him for these amenities. But they really did work hard and he knew that too.

Phillip had to keep all aspects of farm management going smoothly, and he became a hard worker himself. He did not work hard because he enjoyed it, but because he felt a sense of gratitude to Anna for letting him come back and run the farm. He didn't want to let her or Peter down. Phillip was never really capable of love, but the closest thing he felt to love was his feelings for Anna. After all, she was his twin. They had a special bond between them. Anna always knew that Phillip's emotional feelings were not complete. It was like he was able to mimic the actions of showing love and saying the words, but they were empty words. Even Phillip was somewhat saddened by not being able to say that he could love someone. Perhaps it was because he felt that his parents loved Anna more because she came to them first, even if only by a couple of minutes. Phillip always felt that he came in second place with his parents. They were not demonstrative with their love and affection towards him but they were toward Anna. Perhaps this made him feel like a failure of some sort and not worthy of love?

According to Phillip, "men were supposed to be strong and not show much emotion." Perhaps his father felt if he showed Phillip too much love or affection it would make him weak? Anna had picked up on his feelings of inferiority and insecurity throughout the years, and she did everything she could to make him feel he was special and worthy of her love. Phillip knew this deep down and did appreciate it but it didn't change his inner empty feeling of "lovelessness." At a young age he knew and accepted that "alone and empty" would be how he would have to live his life, and although he had hoped for more, he convinced himself that he could live with never having a true love relationship with someone. After all, there were worse things that could have happened to Phillip. He was, after all, born into a financially successful family, he was able to graduate from law school, and he was an attractive man. These were the things that were of the utmost importance to Phillip.

Running the farm was just too much work for one person, so when he had to deal with the hired help, he brought along his farm manager, Al. Al knew the business well. He had worked in the berry industry for years - first for Phillip's parents, then for Anna during the years while Phillip was away, and now he had quite a bit of vineyard acreage of his own. Even though Al had never liked Phillip as a boy and he was quite aware of Phillip's unsavory reputation over the years, he felt lucky to have a job, and the pay was better at the Wilcox farm than at most of the other farms in the area. Since Anna turned over most of the daily farm management to Phillip, she was only involved in the ordering of supplies and keeping up the books; this made it possible for her to devote more of her time to her home in Geneva and to Peter.

Phillip survived the first season and settled in for the cold harsh winter that was around the corner. Although the harvest was over, the really monotonous, grueling work was from November through March, when all of the vines had to be cut back. Phillip spent hours out in the fields trimming in the blustering cold. The only thing that kept him warm was occasionally taking trips back to Buffalo.

Every year brought new berry and grape crops and some new berry-pickers. Most of the workers they had at the Wilcox farm were from Atlanta, New York. It was only around fifteen miles down the road, but it seemed like worlds away.

CHAPTER 5

DURING CARMELITA

As he told me his story, Phillip became calm, especially when he spoke of Carmelita. Although I had learned about their relationship in some of Phillips letters, I never heard these details until now:

Two years had gone by since Phillip had moved back to the farm. He was standing in the kitchen of the big house looking out the window when he saw a new worker walking from the berry-picker house down to the pond. She was by herself, fluttering around like a butterfly, looking at the property gauging what would be expected of her over the next month. Even from that distance Phillip found her absolutely captivating; he couldn't take his eyes off of her. Her hair was an auburn color that seemed to bounce like silk off her well-defined shoulders. Her skin seemed like light milk chocolate and she was very petite. The possibility of being able to tower over her was attractive to Phillip. He couldn't wait to meet her face-to-face but for the first time in his life he was nervous about that first encounter.

Phillip was wondering what was happening to him. He was old enough to be her father but he couldn't stop the warmth that was rising from within. He was conflicted by the sexual stir and simultaneously he yearned to protect this precious little butterfly he saw floating around the grassy area between the big house and the first rows of berries. He didn't know how long he stood there just staring at her but he knew he had to get his growing excitement under control before Flo came into the room.

A school bell was installed into the upper portion of the house and was rung to let the workers know when meals would be served and when breaks could be taken. Even though the workers were not officially on the clock until the next day, Phillip decided that he would ring the bell to summon all of his workers for his standard rundown of the berry picking rules and responsibilities. Phillip washed up and changed into clean farm clothes. Within three minutes, nine berry-pickers lined up by the first row of raspberries: six females and three males. Phillip introduced himself in a stern voice making it very clear that he was only to be addressed as Mr. Wilcox. Only a few of them were the pickers that his parents had used all the years while he was growing up. The rest came on board while he was away at law school in Buffalo or while he was living and practicing law in Canandaigua.

Even though he had encountered some of them before, Phillip asked each of the berry-pickers to identify themselves: Betty, Dorothy, Ruth, Shirley, John, and then came the most beautiful name he had ever heard from a sweet but strong voice. "My name is Carmelita. Thank you for the opportunity to work at your beautiful farm."

The other pickers continued to say their names – Mary, Ritchie and Michael, their foreman. Phillip tried to maintain his composure and authority. Carmelita was so new and fresh. Although all the other women were under thirty, they seemed older and weathered. The berry-pickers named John and Michael were both in their mid-thirties, and Ritchie was Michael's son. They looked after the females – although it was hard to tell whether any of them were married or connected in an intimate way. Phillip liked that about this crew. They were there to work, not socialize or have relations in the berry-picker house. He explained to all of the pickers what was expected of them. The days of the "running of the grapes" had long since passed, and he wasn't going to put up with any of their shenanigans. He made it clear that he was the man in charge.

The next day everyone started the harvest season. Phillip tried to maintain his composure around Carmelita and the other workers. He didn't want it to be obvious that he was falling for a young berry-picking girl with the most stunning, big, brownish-green eyes he had ever seen. Her eyelids opened and closed slowly with such grace and mystique – like a beautiful winter owl's eyes. At first Phillip innocently approached her by making idle chatter when they were picking and crating the berries. It was unusual for Phillip to with mingle with the pickers, but he couldn't help it. He was intrigued and would do anything to spend time with Carmelita.

Phillip quickly learned that Carmelita lived in Atlanta, New York a couple of months out of the year. The rest of the year she lived in New York City. She was not born and raised in Atlanta but she was staying there with her aunts, uncles and cousins in a large cabin with a dorm-like set up. The family all worked at the different farms and vineyards around Canandaigua Lake. What would start off as a berry-picking job for the women would sometimes lead to a little house cleaning or looking after the children. For the men, berry-picking often led to doing odd jobs around the properties. Nothing was too menial for Carmelita's large Italian family. Phillip was captivated by her strong work ethic, especially for such a young girl. Phillip realized that the fact that Carmelita was only sixteen-years old made it legally impossible to be with her in an intimate way – not to mention the morality issue of him still being married to Flo. But where there is a will, Phillip would find a way.

It was on a rainy night close to the end of the first berry harvest when Phillip could no longer resist Carmelita's charms. He didn't know how she would react to his initiation of a kiss or perhaps even more, but when the others went into town for personal supplies, he could no longer resist the attempt. It wasn't the most romantic first encounter but he cleaned up the room in the berry-picker house where the females slept and laid a single hollyhock flower out on the cot for her. Phillip felt like he knew a whole new world of love, and much to his surprise, she seemed truly interested in him, and showed it by making love with him. From that day forward, Carmelita no longer called him Mr. Wilcox.

Normally without the chase, Phillip would not have bothered with her, but things were just so different with Carmelita – everything was fresh and new. True love can melt a frozen heart. All the years of not feeling worthy or capable of love dissipated with their first kiss that night and Phillip Wilcox, former Esquire and now berry-farmer, knew his life was going to change. He felt like his heart had been opened for the first time in his life. Yes, he was actually falling in love. While he truly did enjoy the sexual aspect of their relationship, it wasn't the sex that made him feel special or what he would come to crave. It was Carmelita's loving reaction to him. She was not harsh or critical of anything Phillip would say or do. He did not feel like she was trying to control him or take anything from him. She just welcomed him in every way. This was not anything Phillip had ever experienced in his life. He did not feel like he had to put on false pretenses for her –

he could just be himself. She did not make him feel insecure whatsoever. He was the best man he could be when he was with her and because of her.

Carmelita became Phillip's salvation and, from that moment on, they spent as much time together as possible without being obvious. He was trying to make the short amount of time they would be together as special as possible. Unlike most of the berry-pickers who were there for both the July and September harvests, Carmelita was only to be there for July. She was still in school and had to return to New York City in September when the school year began. She was fortunate in that she was well loved and looked after by her aunts who worked for many years at a shirtwaist shop in Greenwich Village. They let her return to Atlanta for the summers to see her other aunts, uncles and cousins and to make a little extra money for herself.

Phillip and Carmelita would steal away and drive around in Phillip's automobile under the pretense of having to go either into Naples or sometimes even as far away as Geneva to buy farming supplies. They loved listening to the radio when they stopped at little diners along the way. She decided that her favorite song for him was "Somebody Loves Me" by the Henry Lange Baker Hotel Orchestra, and his song for her was "Girl of My Dreams" by the Blue Steele Orchestra with Kenny Sargent. Phillip told me he also recited my song, "Lace Around the Moon," to her and that the words spoke directly to her heart. She felt they were living the words of the song. One of the first times they made love under the large oak tree down by Canandaigua Lake, Carmelita looked up and said, "I see it! I really do see the Lace around the Moon." And she repeated the words from the song:

It all depends on how you look at it

And what you are willing to let your mind's eye see…

All I ask is that you will always think of me.
Whenever you look up and see the lace around the moon,
Know that our hearts will be together soon…

Unfortunately the end of July was upon them and Carmelita had to leave. The night before she left, they took a drive to the Grimes Glen Waterfalls. There they made love and promised each other that every night they were apart they would look up to the moon and remember their hearts would be together soon.

That year, Phillip did not go back to Buffalo; there was no reason. He no longer longed for anyone or anything other than his precious Carmelita. He vowed to wait for her until she returned next year. He thought about going to the New York City to visit her, but how would he explain his absence to Flo or to Anna?

When seventeen-year-old Carmelita came back the next season, they picked up right where they'd left off. As the harvest went on, Phillip noticed that Carmelita was talking more and more to Ritchie and even flirting with him a bit when she didn't think Phillip was around. Ritchie was about twenty, tall, and lean. Phillip didn't like him from the moment he saw him. He thought about letting him go, but those matters were left up to Anna. She relied on different farmers and people who worked in the juice-pressing companies around Canandaigua Lake to do her scouting for her, plus Ritchie's father, Michael, was the foreman of their crew. Phillip couldn't ask Anna to let him go. That would raise too much suspicion.

Ritchie had started to figure out that something might be going on between Phillip and Carmelita, but he really needed this job so he wasn't going to do anything to upset

Mr. Wilcox in any way. Ritchie was the oldest of nine children so his parents desperately needed the money their children worked for and brought back to their small home in Atlanta. Ritchie had wanted bigger and better things for himself, but his sense of family commitment prohibited him from moving away and joining any of the armed forces, which could have been a way out of his monotonous life. He wanted to help his parents and younger siblings before pursuing his own dreams – dreams that had started to include Carmelita.

Phillip and Carmelita continued to spend as much time together as the circumstances would allow. Because Flo could care less about what Phillip did, she never noticed when he wasn't around, but other berry-pickers certainly did start to pick up on what was going on. And Phillip was naive to think that people were not talking and gossiping about him and Carmelita.

Out of respect for Phillip and the fact that she was given special gifts and at times even cash to send back to her aunts, Carmelita was closed-lipped. She saw Phillip as a lost soul and genuinely appreciated his generosity toward her. But what he perceived as her total devotion and love for him might have just been a young girl's crush on an older man. They were not on the same page but were spending as much time as they could in the same bed. Phillip was an eager lover, and Carmelita was an eager participant. He affectionately called her his "little Berry-Princess." She liked the attention – that and the sex bonded them. When that season's harvest came to an end and Carmelita again had to leave, she and Phillip renewed their promise to look up to the moon and know that their hearts would be together soon.

It was a lovely thought, but for a young girl, the cold and lonely winter nights back home in New York City and the equally lonely nights she was spending in Atlanta waiting to start work at the Wilcox farm did not bind their relationship, at least not for her.

Phillip thought he could wait as long as he had to for another moment with Carmelita but this long winter was harder for him to handle than the last. They decided to meet in New York City the week after New Year's. There was a new beautiful hotel called the Essex House that Phillip thought she would absolutely love, and he planned to treat her like his "Berry-Princess." The month before, Phillip told Flo and Anna that he received a letter from Albany notifying him that he needed to go there to straighten out a problem with his law license. Phillip's plan for Carmelita was for her to tell her aunts that she was going out with her friends in Manhattan for a night on the town and that she would be staying at her friend's apartment. Phillip and Carmelita would only be able to have one day and one night together but at least he wouldn't have to wait until July before seeing her again.

Phillip drove his automobile to Rochester where he caught the train to New York City. He arrived at the hotel and prepared the room. Instead of hollyhocks on the bed he laid a single red rose for his love. He also purchased a beautiful dainty charm bracelet, which he placed next to the rose. He had it wrapped in a special box that also included three strands of beautiful glass beads.

As soon as Carmelita arrived, Phillip told her that she was the only one who held a key to his heart and that the bracelet with a key and heart charm was a promissory bracelet to someday marry her. He also told her that the three strands of beads were the most precious things he owned and that a special person in his life gave them to him many years ago – the same person who wrote and sang "Lace Around the Moon." Carmelita did love all of the attention Phillip was adorning her with, and she especially loved the bracelet. It was beautiful, and it was from Tiffany's! She was also surprised to be receiving my beads and was impressed knowing that Phillip had been to New Orleans and knew me. Carmelita wasn't heartless, but she knew that she was going to have to break Phillip's heart.

They ate all of their meals in the hotel room, as Phillip wanted as much time alone with her as possible. He wanted her to have these special moments with him to prove that "he was truly in love with her." Although they made love several times over those twenty-four hours, their time together only reinforced Carmelita's feelings for someone else and for Carmelita, that person was the only one who held the key to her heart. This was a defining moment for both Carmelita and Phillip. Phillip realized Carmelita was the only woman for him and that he wanted to make a life with her, while at the same time Carmelita realized that Phillip was not the man for her. She had no idea how she was going to break the news to Phillip that her and Ritchie had fallen in love. She became so caught up in the moment with all the gifts and attention Phillip was bestowing on her that it just seemed impossible for her to hurt him with the news at that time.

What Phillip didn't know was that Ritchie had taken a train to New York City to see Carmelita for the holidays. Carmelita had planned on telling Phillip it was over between them when he came to visit her but whenever she tried, she just couldn't seem to get it out, so again – Phillip was "let in." When their special time together ended Carmelita returned home to her aunts' apartment and Phillip went back home to the farm.

Having spent this precious time with Carmelita, Phillip was on top of the world and returning without her made him realize he couldn't live without her. He started putting together a plan for their future together…

Carmelita would be eighteen when she came to the berry-picker house for her third season. Phillip would tell Flo that he didn't care whether she would divorce him or not. Either way, he was leaving her to be with Carmelita. He would agree to all of Flo's financial stipulations, and he knew darn well there would be many. This was going to be a very painful slap in her face and Phillip would feel the financial burn. He just wanted out. He wanted to finally be free to be with Carmelita without all of the sneaking around down to the big tree, the Grimes Glen Waterfalls, and the room at the berry-picker house. He didn't care what others would say about him having such a young woman for his new wife.

CHAPTER 6

AFTER CARMELITA

I was afraid of what Phillip was about to tell me and the horror was even worse than I ever could have imagined. By this time, everyone in town had told me their version of this part of the story, but I did my best to now add in Phillip's version as I somehow tried to find compassion for him:

Phillip counted down the days until Carmelita would be arriving. When she finally pulled up in the automobile and gently squirmed out of her seat, he couldn't believe his eyes – Carmelita was with child.

Things were strained around the Wilcox farm. Carmelita kept her distance for the first couple of days and worked at the berry-picking more earnestly than before. Phillip didn't like to go out into the fields if he didn't have to, so that is where Carmelita would stay. By the third day he could no longer stand the silence, and after the workers finished picking the berries for the day, he uncharacteristically gave all of them some extra money to go into Cheshire to get some dinner and pick up some of the personal items they would need for the harvest season. This would give him some special private time with his Carmelita so he could figure out how they were going to tell Flo and Anna about their relationship and their baby. Phillip never let it show or ever spoke about it to anyone but he secretly longed for a child – a healthy child – ever since the death of his unborn child with Flo. His love for Carmelita had softened him, and having a child to carry on his name was very important to him. He kept on thinking that Carmelita was just afraid of coming to him with the news of their baby and that was why she remained so distant, but how wrong he was.

That evening when they were finally alone at the berry-picker house, Carmelita told Phillip she did not love him and that she was starting her own life with Ritchie and their unborn child. She held out the three strands of beads and the bracelet he had given to her and said she could no longer accept these gifts. He was stunned. It took a few minutes to register that what she was telling him was that the child was not his. He felt like someone had punched him in his stomach. How could this be? He truly thought they were in love. He was repulsed by the thought of someone other than him touching Carmelita, making love to her. He snapped in a jealous fit of rage and picked up the first thing he could get his hands on – a large shovel kept close by to ward off intruding wildlife. He couldn't comprehend what she was saying to him and he burst out of control.

Phillip began to hit Carmelita over the head. Although he was sickened by the sound of her skull crushing, he couldn't stop hitting her. The spray of crimson red popped like a firecracker, landing on the walls and all over Phillip's body. His clothes became soaked in blood. He kept on hearing something that sounded like popcorn being popped – it was the sound of the glass beads hitting the ground and breaking as Carmelita crumbled. He suddenly panicked from seeing what was happening. He felt like he was watching it all unfold without his participation. It was like he was watching a silent movie – he didn't fully grasp at that moment he was the main character.

With a few whimpered breaths, Carmelita died in the very same room in which she had signed the wall only two years earlier. Phillip wrapped her in the bed throw, picked up her petite body, and carried her down to the pond by the nut tree, one of the same places they had made love several times before. The very same place where they would lay under the tree and recite "Lace Around the Moon."

He was paralyzed in that spot, cradling Carmelita until the berry-pickers came back from Cheshire, saw all the blood, and realized Carmelita was nowhere to be found. They all ran around the property until Ritchie saw Phillip down at the pond covered in red. As Ritchie got closer, he saw the life he dreamed of derailing before his eyes. The red was Carmelita covered in blood in Phillip's arms.

Everything seemed to be moving in slow motion as Ritchie lunged at Phillip, screaming: "What have you done?" Ritchie quickly checked for a pulse but it was much too late for that. He started pounding his fists on Phillip who did not even try to ward off the punches. Phillip would not let go of Carmelita even though Ritchie tried relentlessly to release his grip. Phillip just sat there incoherently blathering on and on. Within minutes, Carmelita's life had been taken by the unspeakable selfish rage of Phillip Wilcox, Esquire – with his own hands, the now weathered hands of a farmer. Both Phillip and Ritchie were stunned looking at the lifeless body of Carmelita – their true love.

One of the berry-pickers ran back up to the main house and told Flo what had happened and begged that she call for help. In a drunken stupor and slurred speech, unable to grasp what was happening, Flo urged the berry-picker girl to use the phone and call the police herself. It then took over thirty minutes before the police and coroner arrived. Jumping out of their wagons, the deputies rushed down to the tree where they immediately peeled Phillip away from Carmelita. Restrained, Phillip watched with cold eyes as they delicately placed her body on a stretcher and carried her up the hill.

"We are taking you into custody," they said as they made him stand up and placed handcuffs around his wrists, "You are being arrested on the suspicion of the murder of Carmelita Caprizzi."

These words echoed in his mind, but he was somehow unable to comprehend why they were taking him away. He had a look of confusion on his face as he passed the rest of the berry-pickers, who were gathered around in utter disbelief holding onto each other with hopes to offer comfort and gain some in return. They were heartbroken after seeing Carmelita's battered body being carried into the coroner's wagon. Carmelita was family, one of their own. What a waste of such a young and promising life, not to mention the unborn life that was also lost in this unthinkable tragedy.

By this time Anna and Peter arrived at the main house, and were informed of the series of events. Anna, beside herself in shock, asked Peter to take Flo back to his parent's home. She wanted to handle this herself.

Although Anna didn't know Carmelita, she immediately felt an overwhelming, heartfelt sorrow for her. There were a million thoughts going through her head all at once: "How are Carmelita's loved ones going to handle this? How would she tell them? What had provoked Phillip to do such a thing? What would happen to the farm now?

What could she do to make any of this better?"

Suddenly her business sense snapped in, and she knew that she couldn't afford to cancel the harvesting. She went down and spoke with the berry-pickers who were standing outside of the berry-picker house guarded by the deputy who would not allow anyone in. Without knowing what to do, Anna offered the berry-pickers her heartfelt condolences and apologies and let them know that she was just as surprised and stunned as they were by what had happened. They remained speechless. She told them they could stay in the big house and continue working or that she understood if they needed to return home to their families to seek their love and support at this very difficult time. No one responded, but rather just stared blankly at her with disgust.

She took a breath and went into the basement of the big house and broke down. She felt for Phillip but she also felt the weight of the world coming down on her. She truly did love Phillip and felt sorry for him in some way but how selfish and horrific it was for Phillip to do such a thing? Her own brother? She knew he could get out of control in certain ways, but this?

After she composed herself, the first thing she thought to do was to call their family attorney, Charles Watkins, to inform him of the tragedy. She asked him to get down to the local police station as soon as possible and that she would meet him there.

When Phillip arrived at the police station, the deputies took away his blood-soaked clothing, made him put on bathrobe-type sheath, collected samples from under his fingers, took his fingerprints, and gathered samples of blood and hair. Eventually, they brought him food and let him bathe. Phillip slept for six hours that first night. It is interesting how some food, a hot bath, and some sleep can bring a person back to reality. He started comprehending the situation he was in, and in true Phillip fashion, he felt that he too was a victim. He told the head deputy he was going to remain silent and that he wanted to see his lawyer.

Phillip should have done the right thing and confessed to being guilty of this crime right there and then, but instead he started strategizing his defense. Phillip was, after all, an attorney who was very good at manipulating the law. He planned to discuss the plea of "not guilty by reason of temporary insanity" with Charles Watkins.

Phillip remembered learning about a United States congressman who had successfully used this plea for the first time in 1859 after he had killed his wife's lover. And the verdict was not guilty! Phillip felt he could achieve the same outcome: if it was good enough for a congressman, then it was equally good enough for him.

This plea would set the stage for a nationwide attention-grabber. He could become famous and he started to obsess about that possibility. Phillip was okay when he was thinking of these legal matters but when night fell he could think of nothing else other than Carmelita. He was just starting to realize she was gone and he would never be able to hold her, smell her, kiss her. He longed for her. He could cope when they were apart because he always knew he would be seeing her again – but that had all changed. He no longer had Carmelita on earth to love. What had he done?

Charles Watkins realized that what Phillip was going to be facing legally was far outside the realm of his expertise. He knew of a popular but expensive criminal defense attorney practicing in Canandaigua who would be far better equipped to handle Phillip's case. He contacted

Robert "Bulldog" Dupree to see if he could meet Phillip at the police station on Sunday morning. He had already run all of this by Anna to ensure that she was okay with having a local attorney rather than having to pay for someone from out of town representing Phillip. Phillip didn't have anywhere near the amount of money his defense was going to cost. Anna would have to be willing to pay for most of it. Although she understood the fuller story now, she was still willing to do this for her brother – her twin.

Robert "Bulldog" Dupree was dapperly dressed when he met with Phillip and Charles Watkins at the local police lock-up Sunday morning. As it turned out, "Bulldog" attended the University of Buffalo Law School for some of the same years Phillip was there. They had known of one another, but did not exactly travel in the same circles. While Phillip's parents were prosperous, Bulldog's parents were far beyond that – they were wealthy and hobnobbed with politicians and the very affluent throughout New York State and all over the country. The Dupree family had the largest vineyard on Canandaigua Lake – 90 acres – including a harvesting business, pie-making business and their own grape-pressing business. They were the "Berry-Kings" of the region. Robert received his undergraduate degree from Fresno State, which had a unique on-campus raisin and grape vineyard and a commercial winery. Since his family was entrenched in their vineyard and their wine and grape businesses, they thought it would be prudent to send Robert to a college where he could use his wits to learn more about the wine industry. While working on his business degree, he found the time to play football for Fresno State's Bulldogs. He was steady on his feet and had great stamina. Although he was just medium sized, he had great strength. He was a linebacker and boy could he run! Hence, when he graduated with his degree, his fellow classmates gave him the nickname of Bulldog, and it stayed with him ever since.

Phillip shook hands with Bulldog and thanked him for agreeing to take him on as a client. When they discussed their defense strategy, Phillip was very pleased that Bulldog immediately brought up the possibility of pleading not guilty by reason of temporary insanity. Although Phillip felt he was a perfect specimen of a man and that a mental defect was not possible, pleading not guilty by temporary insanity (a crime of passion) was something he could accept, especially if it meant he would not be imprisoned for as many years as he would be if he were found guilty. The other possibility was that Phillip could plead guilty but use an insanity defense. This, however, could result in several years in a mental institution, which could possibly last longer than the prison sentence he could receive. If he went that road, there would not even be a trial, and Phillip felt he deserved "his day in court." He realized this was all a gamble with his life but at least now Phillip and his attorney were on the same page.

Only Phillip, Bulldog, Anna, Charles, the D.A., and two deputies were allowed in the courthouse for the arraignment. Judge Thomas Clark was presiding. The little courthouse was very weathered on the outside, and the inside was not much better. Paint was chipping on many of the walls and parts of the ceiling were buckled in from years of heavy snow accumulation. There were water stains all over the walls, and the place had a musty odor to it. The county did not have money in their budget for repairs so business just went on as usual, and the people who had to come to the courthouse tried not to stay for too long. This courthouse had never seen such a high profile arraignment.

Bulldog and Phillip hardly had the time to go over last-minute items before the two deputies escorted them to the courthouse. Phillip was put into handcuffs, but escaping was the furthest thing from his mind. He was very confident that he was going to be proven not guilty by reason of temporary insanity, so he looked at it all as a formality. He needed to know what was going to become of him. He couldn't stand not knowing what his future would be or where he would be spending it. Although Phillip felt tormented by all the recent events, he still believed that he could go on and have a normal, full life. He now knew what it felt like to love and it was the best feeling he had ever experienced. He hoped to have this feeling again in his life. Unfortunately, it would not be with Carmelita, the one person he truly loved.

The laws allowed for those being charged to either enter a plea at the arraignment or wait until the initial trial appearance. The defense decided they would do it at the arraignment, and when the judge said to Phillip, "You are being charged with manslaughter in the second degree. How do you plead?" Phillip replied, "I plead not guilty by reason of temporary insanity."

Neither the judge nor the district attorney saw this coming. They were bewildered. They were aware of this possible plea, but this was small-town America, and it was never used before in the township of Naples or in all of Ontario County. Bulldog knew that it had never been used anywhere in that entire region, and he was banking on that fact. He wanted this to all be unfamiliar to the prosecution as he felt that could give him and Phillip a better chance of using it to their advantage.

Bulldog asked for Phillip to be released on his own recognizance. The judge denied the request and set the bail at $40,000. Phillip and Anna gasped. That was not going to be possible. They did not have that kind of money, and he certainly couldn't ask Flo for it. She wanted nothing to do with Phillip for a long time, and after the arrest she had only distanced herself from him further. Phillip and Anna had discussed that she could contribute $10,000, but she was not willing to sell the farm or put it up for collateral. She loved her brother but would not give up the one thing she worked towards her entire life. Besides, she still had to keep the farm up and running to bring in the money to sustain the place and pay for his legal fees, which were certain to increase. This entire responsibility fell on Anna's shoulders. To Anna, the fact that Phillip was her twin made it impossible for her not to help him. She had to take care of him, but she was still married and did not want the marriage to suffer anymore than it already had as a result of the situation. She would not go to Peter for the money; she just couldn't.

News traveled fast in the small neighboring towns around Naples, Canandaigua, and Geneva and much shame was brought to Peter and Florence's reputable family. To them, Phillip was a monster who ruined their daughter's life and put a cloud of suspicion around them. Bottom line - Phillip Wilcox, Esquire would have to spend the next several months locked up. Needless to say, Phillip was not happy about this situation. Irate, in fact. And that's where I was asked to come in.

The press dubbed it the "Berry-Picker Murder." Although there were more high-profile murder trials taking place across the nation and the Lindbergh kidnapping was all anyone could talk about, people from neighboring cities were coming to get a glimpse of the berry-picker house. They would also sit outside of the local police station with hopes of seeing Anna or Phillip's attorney. These two were becoming small-town celebrities but for all the wrong reasons. Anna wanted nothing to do with this invasion of her privacy. On the other hand, Bulldog welcomed any and all press. He wanted to keep Phillip's upcoming trial on the tongues of anyone who would wag them. Murder is good for small-town business – this was the best thing that ever happened to Naples' economy. The few hotels in town were booked solid. Townspeople even started taking reservations from different press people and tourists who were going to be coming back for the actual trial. They were planning on renting out rooms in their homes so they could make some extra money. This was the largest influx of people Naples had ever seen.

Much preparatory work needed to be done. Witnesses for both the prosecution and defense had to be interviewed, and much legal haggling had to be worked out before the actual trial. The district attorney's office would be hiring a psychiatrist from Canandaigua to try and prove that Phillip was not temporarily insane. Bulldog hired a psychiatrist from Rochester that he would be calling to testify that Phillip could have been temporarily insane at the time of the murder. It was the prosecution's burden to prove Phillip's guilt and they needed to establish that fact beyond a reasonable doubt. Phillip's psychiatrist wouldn't be able to testify that he was legally insane at the time of the murder, as he had no idea of Phillip's mental condition at that time. However, they were hoping that the psychiatrist would be able to provide medical proof that Phillip could have had mental illness temporarily. Phillip would have to be evaluated, and both sides wanted to get that out of the way as soon as possible. This was going to be another expense that would be added to Phillip's increasing legal fees. So far Anna was able to keep up on the bills, but with every passing day it was getting more difficult. The district attorney's office was moving full-steam forward with the trial, which was set for the beginning of December.

When I arrived, the whole town was in a state of limbo for the four months leading up to the trial. The newspaper writers interviewed local business people and just about anyone who was willing to discuss the upcoming trial. They were looking for dirt, but mud was what they found. Gossip about the Berry-Picker Murder was editorialized in many regional tabloids and newspapers and even made its way to New York City.

The sad part was people were more wrapped up in Phillip's trial and the Wilcox farm than they were concerned about the family of Carmelita and the tragedy that Phillip inflicted upon her and her unborn child. Carmelita somehow became incidental to the story despite the fact that her death was the reason the story was being written. But it is the harsh reality that money talks and makes people talk – and so they were talking about Phillip and not Ritchie.

Ritchie had lost his love and his unborn child. It only upset him further that people seemed to be more interested in Phillip being found not guilty than they were in seeing justice served. He did not like being reminded that Phillip had been intimate with Carmelita when he was trying so hard to continue to believe that it had been over between them. Carmelita had told him that she loved him and that they would plan a life together. Ritchie knew Carmelita had chosen him over Phillip; nevertheless he couldn't help but grow more jealous and angry as the days went on.

CHAPTER 7

THE TRIAL

Gossip continued to spread throughout town about what had happened and what would happen. Usually people avoid jury duty but not in this case. People considered themselves lucky if they were selected for the Berry-Picker Murder. It took over three days to select all of the jurors and alternates. It was so odd. Over the time that I spent there, Phillip was becoming less despised and more of a local celebrity… or should I say "a curiosity." Although he asked about it often, I tried to keep Phillip sheltered from the outside world and focused on what he could do to find peace. I didn't want to see him suffer for years sitting in prison, but I honestly didn't know how he would ever go on living after this. There seemed no solution to the way this tragedy had unfolded. It only seemed to become more complex with each passing moment:

The trial started with much excitement and anticipation. Nothing happened until noon, as workers prepared the courthouse to accommodate the large number of people who were going to be in attendance. It was interesting that the county found the money to make all of the improvements to the courthouse. It was given a complete overhaul before the trial began. The musty smell was replaced with the smell of fresh paint. It wasn't perfect but it was a far cry compared to the way it looked during the arraignment. Many conjectured it would be a lengthy, drawn-out trial. That morning the local farmers farmed, the local berry-pickers trimmed back vines, the local businessmen tended to their factories, and the local women prepared meals. Everyone finished what they needed to do so that when noon came, they could stand outside the courthouse to see the press, local politicians and the other people who were "lucky enough" to get a seat inside, enter the building. They were especially waiting for the families of Carmelita and Ritchie to arrive.

Only a few seats were available for the everyday folk who showed up out of their own morbid curiosity and they were on a first-come, first-serve basis. People actually camped out in front of the courthouse the night before so that they could get a coveted seat inside. A row of seats was left open for Carmelita and Ritchie's families.

Carmelita's two aunts returned from New York City for the trial. They had been completely heartbroken since learning of Carmelita's death. They looked after Carmelita as if she was their own daughter for most of her life, and they wanted to see justice for her senseless death. They wanted Phillip to be given the maximum sentence, and even that was not enough punishment in their minds. They wanted Phillip to "rot in hell" but not before spending as many years behind bars as the law would allow. They entered the courthouse with their heads hanging and hands over their faces to avoid any questions from the press.

When Phillip entered, he looked exhausted and quite small in his suit. During the time I was there, he had lost several pounds. Even so, he held his head high and made eye contact with anyone who looked at him. He was composed on the outside but I could tell he was anxious on the inside. When he saw me across the room, he didn't exactly smile but it was more a look of utter appreciation and gratitude. We shared a moment between us that did both of our hearts good before the judge pounded his gavel and the long-awaited trial officially began.

The district attorney for Ontario County was prosecuting the case. He was a forward-thinking man by the name of Francis P. Murphy. He assigned a woman, Molly McGuire, to be his co-counsel. To choose a woman was highly unusual at this time, but he knew what he was doing. The papers dubbed them the M&M Team. Phillip detested them. Not only because they were prosecuting him but Francis was only a couple of years older than him and both Francis and Molly were quite a bit taller than him. Molly purposely wore high-heels to make Phillip feel uncomfortable.

After the prosecution and the defense went through their opening remarks, the prosecution went into Carmelita and Phillip's love affair by calling two of the berry-pickers to testify that they did indeed see Carmelita and Phillip participating in an adulterous affair. Phillip had no idea that whenever he and Carmelita were down by the pond or the tree making love, there were always eyes or ears taking it all in. The prosecution needed to prove to the jury that it was indeed Phillip who killed Carmelita, and by establishing that they were having an affair, it strengthened their case. They wanted to affirm that no one else had motive to kill Carmelita other than Phillip. After all, he believed that Carmelita had done him wrong by telling him that she was leaving him to be with Ritchie and start her life with their unborn child. Phillip's defense had the right to cross-examine, but Bulldog opted for "no further questions" after each of the witnesses took the stand. There was no point in debating their words. Bulldog was not trying to prove that Phillip didn't kill Carmelita, only that he had done so because he was temporarily insane at the time he did it. Bulldog attempted to convince the jury that Phillip had lost control of himself when he killed Carmelita because he couldn't handle what she told him and so he lashed out at the first thing he could and that was Carmelita. Actually, the defense's tactics helped to substantiate that Phillip and Carmelita were involved. The jurors had been instructed before the trial began that they were to try and remain silent and not show outward signs of how they were feeling at hearing any of the witnesses' statements, but you could see on the faces of some of them that they felt utter distain towards Phillip. The reporters were taking this all in as if it were music to their ears. People just seemed to be feeding on this "scandal," and the more drama and upset that the reporters could include, the more their newspapers would sell.

The M&M Team planned to unfold all of their evidence layer by layer. They spent the last four months preparing for the trial by using private investigators to dig into Phillip's life and find out as much information as they could to strengthen their case. Now that they proved to the jury that Carmelita and Phillip were involved, they zeroed in on the most critical elements of their prosecution and their next witness.

Seeming reluctant, Kay Fletcher approached the bench and was directed to sit in the witness box. Phillip didn't think he recognized her. She must have been in her late-thirties. Maybe she worked on the farm at one time? As soon as she sat down, D.A. Murphy asked her how she knew the defendant. When she paused, he reminded her that she was under oath. She took a breath and began to explain that as a young woman she had worked for the Wilcox's as a berry-picker and stayed in the berry-picker house for many harvests. She went on to reveal that nineteen years ago, her best friend Angela Caprizzi (GG), confided in her that she had gotten pregnant by Phillip Wilcox and that she was moving to New York City to have her baby.

Everyone in the courtroom gasped and Phillip turned and looked at me. I couldn't believe that he would have left this part out of his story. Looking at his face now, I realized that, along with everyone else in the room, this was the first time that he was ever hearing this news.

"The next year, I visited GG and her baby in New York City," continued the witness.

"Yes? Go on…" D.A. Murphy seemed calm, cool, and collected and ready to deliver the next blow, but as everyone in the courtroom drew closer to the edge of their seats, the witness was becoming more and more uncomfortable. "What was the name of the baby, Ms. Fletcher?" he prompted.

"The baby's name was…" she swallowed as if she was about to drop a bomb on the entire city. "The baby's name was… Carmelita."

The courtroom went wild!

Bulldog stood up yelling "Objection – hearsay!"

The judge slammed down his gavel: "Sustained."

By this time the witness was in tears while she kept on rambling on. The damn had been broken and now it was all coming out: "GG begged me to never tell anyone any of this as it would prohibit her from receiving financial support for her and her daughter. I never intended on telling anyone this information as I knew it would hurt many people and I never wanted that guilt on my conscience but the private investigator who came to my house told me I had to tell what I knew."

Bulldog screamed out, "Judge... can we please recess until tomorrow morning so that we have time to go over this information?" The judge saw no other recourse than to do exactly that as the entire courtroom was out of control and he couldn't seem to keep them quiet.

Finally he made his voice heard over the roar of the crowd: "Court adjourned until tomorrow morning." He also reminded the jurors that they were not to discuss this matter with their families, the press, or anyone. He told the D.A. Murphy and Bulldog to meet him in his chambers immediately.

Once they were behind closed doors, Bulldog said that since he had no prior knowledge that they would be calling Kay Fletcher as a witness and what she said was hearsay, that this should be grounds for a mistrial. The judge was not willing to grant a mistrial at this point. However, he did agree that in the morning he would instruct the jurors to disregard the statements that Ms. Fletcher made. They would be inadmissible. But the damage had already been done – there was no going back from this point.

The deputies brought Phillip back to the lock-up and he looked totally confused. He was trying to comprehend everything that just went down in court. After meeting in the judge's chambers, Bulldog asked Charles Watkins to go with him later that afternoon to see Phillip. When they arrived, Charles realized he had no other alternative other than to tell Phillip all of the things his parents never wanted him to know or that Charles ever wanted to tell anyone: "It turns out that while you were away at law school, and GG discovered she was pregnant, she went to your parents for hush money. Of course, there wasn't any way to prove that GG's child was yours, but your parents had no reason not to believe GG. They knew what you were up to and with whom. And, either way, they did not want to take the risk of her going around town and telling everyone that she was having your child, so – for her promising that she would never say a word to anyone, not even her parents – they gave her $10,000."

Phillip was breathing heavily at this point. It all became clear to him at that moment. He said, "All those years ago at the reading of my parent's will, the initials A.C. were for Angela Caprizzi! It was GG that was left the $10,000 in their will?" Charles avoided Phillip's eyes when he responded – "Yes Phillip, you are correct. They made GG take this secret with her to her grave, which she did."

"Except for Kay Fletcher?"

"Correct again Phillip – except for Kay Fletcher."

How could his parents never have told him? He had a child? And was that child, in fact, Carmelita? No, it couldn't be.

Phillip was stunned, crushed, depleted, and repulsed. How could it be that Carmelita was his daughter? All the time he was in love with her, she might have been his daughter? This all felt so unjust to him. All he had cared about since meeting Carmelita, since first making love to Carmelita, was the future he had hoped to have with her. She had become his everything – his reason for getting up in the morning, his reason for smiling at night when he would go to sleep. She was in his heart and in his dreams. He was now reliving the anguish of what he had done to his one true love and now finding out she could possibly have been his daughter – how could this all be? He didn't want to believe it.

This was all becoming too much for him to handle and he was beginning to break down. He asked Charles and Bulldog to let him be alone and please leave. He needed to let everything sink in so that he could regain his composure. Also, he asked them to please see if I would come to see him.

When they found me they said he was desperate so I went right away, but the deputies wouldn't let me in until later that evening.

"Sit down, my friend," he said as I pulled the chair in front of the cell. "You are my only salvation now."

As he began to cry, I somehow knew that this would be our last confessional.

He explained to me that he initially thought that Kay could have been lying but that now he knew it was all true. That he felt it in his heart. "I killed my daughter," he said looking me straight in the eyes. "I did that. I did all of it."

And then he began to sob. I wanted so much to reach out and hug him and give him my shoulder to cry on, but the cell doors made that impossible. I took hold of his fingers in mine through the slots while he continued to cry and cry and I let him. He was crying for Carmelita and he was crying for life itself. For all the ways it had gone. For what he knew and what he didn't know. For all he regretted. For how he couldn't ever go back. No other words were spoken between us and eventually the deputies came in and told me I had to leave.

The next day things proceeded along in court. As previously discussed the day before, the judge instructed the jurors to disregard the statements that Ms. Fletcher made. The prosecution called the coroner from New York City to the bench and swore him in. In the small town of Naples, there was not a certified coroner who had the expertise needed. The coroner explained that he had used a new kind of testing that was able to show common proteins in the blood.

"Carmelita's unborn child was a baby boy," said the coroner, "And most likely was Phillip Wilcox's child."

There were gasps and confusion on every face in the room – even the judge's. Bulldog didn't have it in him to object. Phillip gasped for air.

Everyone was trying to take this all in and were not paying much attention when Ritchie ran up to where Phillip was seated and in a sudden fit of rage plunged his trimming shears into Phillip's back. "A life for a life!" he screamed. For a few moments, everything seemed to freeze as deep red blood began to flow out from the bottom of Phillip's suit onto the floor. Horrified and in shock, Anna and I ran to Phillip. We knew that today's outcome would probably not be good but we had no idea it would end like this. Phillip was dazed, confused, and gasping for breath. "I'm sorry Carmelita," he kept saying over and over again, "I'm sorry, Carmelita... I love you so much. Please believe me. I love you so much..."

One of the deputies drew his gun and pointed it at Ritchie, telling him to get down on his knees and put his hands up.

Bulldog, being the consummate attorney that he was, turned to Ritchie and whispered, "Do not say a word. When they take you to the lock-up, demand that you be allowed to see your attorney. You are going to need a good attorney, and I just happen to know of one who may be available."

One of the fast-thinking deputies had called for an ambulance wagon, but it took over ten minutes for them to arrive. By then it was too late to save Phillip. Just before he took his final breath, Phillip looked at me and smiled. "When you look up and see the lace around the moon…"

He was trying to finish but his life was fading before my eyes. He fell to the ground and just as he had held Carmelita, I held him now.

"I know," I said through my tears holding his head in my lap, "Know that our hearts will be together soon."

EPILOGUE

Anna was heartbroken at having to bury her brother. She was now a lone twin. Believe me, Anna was not oblivious to Phillip's indiscretions and sins but he was her brother – her fraternal twin brother – and I knew she would mourn his death for quite some time. She said what would keep her going was to focus on her marriage with Peter. She shared that they wanted to start a family and for her sake, I hoped that dream would come true. She could only imagine how odd it was going to be to go on living without Phillip. Anna was a strong woman and I knew she was going to be okay. She was just going to need to surround herself with as much love as possible.

Anna had a small burial ceremony for Phillip down by the nut tree a week after Phillip was killed. It was only Anna, Bulldog, Charles Watkins and myself that gathered round. Anna hired two men to dig the grave and place his casket into the ground. He was buried right next to the place where he last held Carmelita. Anna felt that would be the best place for Phillip to be.

When the brief ceremony ended, Anna went into her pocketbook and pulled out a handful of shards of glass beads – the very same beads I gave to Phillip so many years ago in New Orleans. She gently laid these broken pieces on top of the casket, and we all had a silent moment before the gravediggers shoveled dirt to cover the casket.

I stayed in Naples long enough to see Anna through this very difficult time. On my last day at the Wilcox farm, just before Anna took me to my train, I went down to the berry-picker house. As I entered, I saw Phillip's whole life story playing before my eyes. So many parts I wished I could change. Even though Phillip did many terrible things in his life, I still wanted to love him.

I looked at the wall of all those who signed their names over the years. I ran my hand over the sweet words of Angela and Carmelita.

Then, without thinking, I took out a pencil and began to write on the wall myself. I never could find the words to tell Phillip exactly why I felt such a strong connection to him all these years. The reason was just something too profoundly sad to me and I could never say these words before because then it would make my truth so real: "Phillip, many years ago, I had a son that I chose to give up. When I met you, it was somewhat like meeting my own son. Over the years and through our letters, you became the son that I had never had the pleasure of knowing. I will hold your memory close to my heart. Just as you had taken my hand to your heart back in New Orleans so many years ago – it is when you take another's hand to your heart, forever now, we'll never part."

AFTERWORD

As I explained at the beginning of this story, it is fictional. However, I intertwined fiction and non-fiction throughout to incorporate different experiences I have had throughout my own life. For example, Pierre, the jazz singer from New Orleans, the narrator of the story, is me in some ways. My middle name is Pierre, and my love of New Orleans has been a guiding force in many aspects of my life. I have always felt a connection to New Orleans even before I ever went there. I would read books about NOLA and longed for all of the experiences I imagined it would have. When I finally did visit for the first time, I felt like I belonged there – I was home. I realize not everyone can identify with my love for New Orleans or feel the same way I feel about it. I get that it is not everyone's cup of tea - or should I say "cup of Café Du Monde's coffee?" But if you do love and embrace New Orleans the way I do, you can't shake it. I relive my NOLA experiences daily.

As I finished writing this novella, I was on a plane to NOLA. I wanted to experience it again so that I could think about the story as I walked the streets. With fresh thoughts and experiences – I knew the story would be from my NOLA heart. The best way I can explain the feeling I get each time I go there is a quote from a song - "To be living in a moment you would die for." After all, with every waking moment that we are fortunate to be living, we are just creating our lifetime memories. Most of my fondest memories are NOLA-heart-driven.

"Lace Around the Moon" came to me one August evening when all of my nine siblings and their spouses and children were in town for my father's and my surprise birthday party. I sat under a tree gazing up at the moon. Looking up at the sky through the tree's leaves, it looked like the moon had lace around it, and the words to the song came to me. "Lace Around the Moon" became a love song that reconnects people. I knew someday, somehow, someway I would use it for something – I just didn't know when until now.

No one knows what that future will hold. For all of us with health, hope and a plan there can be a future. Phillip did have a plan for his; however, because of his actions, not only was his future derailed but so were the lives of so many others with whom he was involved. Although this story is fictional, it is pertinent to all of our lives. Think before you act - or live or die with the consequences.

.

ABOUT THE AUTHOR

Mary Pierre Quinn-Stanbro is from Buffalo, NY and currently resides there. She is the oldest of ten children from a very close knit Irish Catholic family. She is married to Gene Stanbro and will move to their Gene-Pierre Vineyard in Naples, NY when she retires from her Federal Government career where she has provided thirty-one years of public service. Mary Pierre is currently co-writing her next Novella called "The Band of Blue" with her sisters. It is about a fictional murder that takes place in Buffalo back in the late 1950's. It is a dedication to the Buffalo Police Department and her father and grandfather who were both Buffalo Police Officers. She also is working on a prequel to the *Berry-Picker House* entitled *Lace Around the Moon.* Mary Pierre has an Associate's Degree from Trocaire College and a Bachelor's Degree from Buffalo State College. She started writing short stories and poems in grammar school, and she has always wanted to share her writing with others.

MARY PIERRE QUINN-STANBRO

Made in the USA
Columbia, SC
15 June 2018